1

It's Ok To Tell

Gyfted Ink LLC

Books may be purchased by contacting the publisher and author at:

gyftedink@gmail.com

Publisher: Gyfted Ink, a division of Gyfted Ink, LLC

Editor: Melissa Henry Stover

Creative Consultant: To God be the glory

Library of Congress Catalog Number: 2015907143

{Gyfted Ink LLC} {Lugoff, SC}

ISBN- 13: 978-0692430699

ISBN 10: 0692430695-

1. Young Adult 2. Children

First Edition

Printed in United State⬚

IT'S OKAY TO TELL

MELISSA HENRY STOVER

Susan loved going to her grandma's house. She always had fun. Her and grandma would bake cookies and go shopping. She would always get to choose where they would eat lunch, and grandma always brought her favorite ice cream strawberry. She kissed her mom and dad good

bye , and ran into the house without a glance back. Her mom always worried about her but knew she was safe with her mom.

4

Susan had a great time at grandmas and was excited to go to school and give her teacher some of the cookies her and grandma had made. Ms. Williams always looked forward to her fresh baked cookies. She would never tell anyone but Susan was her favorite student, always happy and always smiling. Susan noticed that they had a stranger in the room that day.

The stranger looked almost like her grandma. The teacher introduced her and said that everyone should pay attention. Susan sat very still and listened to every word. The nice lady started telling them about Emily a little girl who was their age. Each weekend Emily would go to her Grandparents house and she loved going there until her cousin Tony came to live there. Tony always wanted to hug Emily and kiss on her, this made Emily very uncomfortable.

Then one day Tony touched Emily under her clothes, and told her it was their secret. Emily knew that touching her there was wrong, even though Tony had told her if she told no one would believe her, , she knew that she had to tell someone. Her grandma believed her and called the police. They took Tony away and he never touched Emily again.

Susan enjoyed hearing the story about Emily. After school Susan told her teacher that she had something to tell her. Susan shared a big secret with her teacher. Her teacher told her how brave she was and that she was very proud of her for sharing it with her. Now that Mr. Green, her grandmas neighbor was in jail Susan enjoyed going to her grandma's house more than ever. Susan had the courage to tell her teacher that he had been touching her for a very long time. It's ok to tell if someone is touching you in private places, or asking you to touch them. Remember its ok to tell.

Jimmy hit a home run. Everyone stood up and cheered as he ran around the bases. His mom yelled the loudest he could hear her voice over everyone. Jimmy always loved seeing his mom happy. After the game the team had pizza as usual and the coach invited everyone over for a sleepover to celebrate the big win.

Jimmy's mom had to work so she didn't have a problem with him going. She kissed Jimmy goodbye and she told him she would pick him up the next morning. The next morning Jimmy was very quiet. He told his mom that he didn't feel good and he went straight to bed. His mom was worried because Jimmy never got sick.

He stayed in his room all day and he didn't even eat dinner and his mom had made his favorite tacos. Later on that night she heard Jimmy crying she went into his room and held him until he stopped crying. When she asked him what was wrong he said nothing and just stared at the floor. His mom held his hand and told him that there wasn't anything too bad to tell her, and that they could fix anything together.

As Jimmy began to tell his mom what happened she just hugged him and told him how proud she was of him and how brave he was. Jimmy told his mom that the coach had touched him and made Jimmy do things that he didn't want to do. He told Jimmy that if he told that he would hurt him and his mom. Jimmy's mom called the police and they came right away.

After talking to Jimmy , they went to the coach's house and they arrested him. Because of Jimmy other kids came forward and admitted that the coach had did the same thing to them. He was put in jail for a very long time and he wasn't able to ever hurt Jimmy or his friends again. Don't believe someone if they threaten to hurt you or your family. They want to make you afraid because they know if you tell that they will be in big trouble. Remember it's ok to tell.

12

Anna hated going over to her grandma's house. She loved her grandma very much but she hated her older cousin Casey. Casey's parents put her out because she was getting into so much trouble. Grandma couldn't stand the thought of Casey being on the street so she let her come live with her until she could get on her feet.

Every time that Anna was scheduled to go to her grandma's, she would try to talk her mom out of taking her. Her mom would always ask her why and then Anna would just say never mind. Anna loved her grandma but she had to figure out a way to make them see that Casey should not be there.

14

Casey made Anna touch her, and she would touch Anna in her private parts. She told Anna that no one would ever believe her and that Grandma wouldn't love her anymore. Casey would come in the bathroom while Anna took her bath, she would tell grandma that she was washing Anna's back, but she would be touching Anna and it made Anna very uncomfortable.

Tonight when she came in her room Anna had a plan and if it worked she would never have to worry about Casey touching her ever again. When Casey came in her room Anna was ready. Casey began to tell Anna where to touch her at, and what to do. Reluctantly Anna did as she was told.

Then all of a sudden the room door swung open and Anna's parents were there with the police. Anna called her mother on the phone and when Casey came into the room she did not hang up the phone up the just slid it under the cover. Her parents heard everything that was going on. Anna was glad that they lived only two blocks away, which is why they were able to get there so quickly. The police arrested Casey and took her to jail. The police told Anna that she was a brave young lady. Her parents hugged her tight and promised they would never let anyone hurt her again. Never let anyone touch you male or female it's wrong. Remember its ok to tell.

Randy's dad was the best. He loved living with his dad. He saw his mom a lot. She only lived about a mile away. Randy loves living with his dad because they get to do a lot of guy things together. His mom was a flight attendant, so she traveled a lot. It was ok, the only time he was sad was when his dad had to go out of town for work. It wasn't often but Randy wish that it never happened. His old babysitter moved, and he really didn't like the new one.

He just didn't feel comfortable around her. She was always walking in the bathroom on him, and acting as if she didn't know that he was in there. She was very weird. This time his dad would be gone for the weekend and he hated that Margo would be staying there. At least his dad had said that it was ok if his friend Rob stayed with him while he was gone.

The boys were in the room playing the video game when Margo came in and started dancing in front of them. Randy asked her to leave and finally she did. They played the game until the both fell asleep. Randy woke up and Margo was lying beside him, she told him that it was ok, she began touching him, and he was very uncomfortable. He asked her to leave or that he would scream. Margo left and the next day Randy just ignored her.

That Sunday there was a knock on the door, it was the police and Randy's mom. Rob wasn't asleep and he heard everything that happened. He called his mom and told her what happened and then she called Randy's mom. Randy was so happy to have a good friend like Rob, he didn't know what to do. If you know that your friend is being touched, or that someone is doing something to them please tell an adult. Remember its ok to tell.

Melissa Henry Stover is a published author, a business owner, and a motivational speaker. Life has thrown her some punches, but she has managed to stay afloat and use those obstacles to help other people along the way. Melissa loves reading, writing and helping anyone she can. Melissa has two sons Thedrin & Marcus a beautiful granddaughter that she affectionately calls Skye and a beautiful Angel in Heaven her daughter Carissa Grace who encourages her every step of the way. Melissa resides in South Carolina.

This book is also in loving memory Of Carissa Grace Stover, and every child that has lost their life or lived with childhood asthma.

A GYFTED INK PRODUCTION

OTHER BOOKS BY

MELISSA HENRY STOVER

MONKEYS TASTE LIKE CHOCOLATE (TATE PUBLISHING)

TO GOD BE THE GLORY

24

www.ingramcontent.com/pod-product-compliance
Lightning Source LLC
Chambersburg PA
CBHW061800040426
42447CB00011B/2391

9 7 8 0 6 9 2 4 3 0 6 9 9